LEAD FOR IMPACT

Why mindfulness, empathy, and psychological safety don't make great leaders

By

Dr. Chris McAlister

With Bret Burchard

Printed in the United States of America.
First paperback edition: May 2024

Paperback: 979-8-9859869-3-8
Hardcover: 979-8-9859869-4-5
eBook: 979-8-9859869-5-2
Audiobook: 979-8-9859869-6-9

Written and edited by: Dr. Chris McAlister and Bret Burchard
Cover art by: Brave Little Beast

TABLE OF CONTENTS

FOREWORD

In April of 2019 Chris McAlister sent me an email out of the blue. The subject line was, "Yo".

This is what the email said:

> *My name is Chris McAlister. We're connected on Instagram. I saw something you posted on identity a while back. Identity is a particular interest of mine and focus of my work. It would be fun to connect.*

So, we scheduled a phone call and jumped right into the deep end.

I paced around my neighborhood for over an hour as we covered psychology, leadership, business, insecurities, and growth. Chris' knowledge in the space of human development is *extensive*. We immediately connected over our shared desire to see leaders and teams transform in deep, meaningful ways. We were both annoyed by the same old inspirational training that regurgitated the latest self-development books. We lamented that most support for leaders was surface-level and failed to help them understand why they might be stuck and what shifts they needed to make to move forward.

When the phone call ended, I realized that I was very far away from home and couldn't remember how I got there. The conversation was *that good.*

Since then Chris and I have had many more conversations about helping leaders understand themselves so they can more effectively serve their teams. We've co-hosted events together and I jump at any chance to collaborate with him. I've benefited immensely from his coaching, wisdom, and mentorship. Along the way we've developed a deep and generative friendship for which I'm very grateful.

The gift of learning from Chris hasn't been limited to interactions with him alone. He surrounds himself with fantastic people like Bret Burchard, whose fingerprints and wisdom are all over this book and many others. The movement they're building at SightShift reflects not only a desire to create a vehicle for personal growth – for the SightShift team, their certified coaches and clients – but also to push people a little deeper than they might be comfortable, into the challenging work of true transformation.

Thank goodness.

Because the gaggle of leadership influencers and countless management podcasts won't create the kind of leaders we need in the world today. We don't need performers as leaders who spend more time posting about their role than supporting their team. We don't need authoritarians scrambling for control or pacifists too afraid to chart a course. We need leaders fueled by a different source of motivation than the validation so many leaders unconsciously crave.

We need leaders who lead for impact.

When Chris first told me about the concept for this book, it was all I could think about for weeks. *Of course, this makes so much sense!* I thought. Once you see it you can't unsee it. In every organization you'll see leaders who are confused about what matters most; and if you're honest with yourself you'll see how, you too, can miss the mark when you forget what it means to prioritize impact above anything else.

Thankfully, *Lead for Impact* is a guiding light for any leader who is willing to take a hard look at their inner world and admit that maybe, just maybe, the thing holding them back from a greater sense of peace, selflessness, fulfillment and impact is the fact that they're asking for something from their leadership role that their leadership role can't give them.

If we want to make an impact in our little corner of the world as we lead others, we've got to find a way to turn the volume down on our need for external affirmation *and* we must acquire the awareness to understand our unique gifts and blindspots.

This book will help you do all that, and then some.

Reagan Pugh
Author & Speaker
Austin, Texas – May 2024

PART 1

INSECURE LEADERS ARE RUINING THE WORLD

CHAPTER 1
THE TWO LEADERSHIP PATHS

The notification hit his phone at 7 p.m.

Sam groaned in frustration.

He retreated to his home office, leaving his wife and two kids to enjoy dinner without him again.

It wasn't supposed to be like this.

Sam had worked his way to CEO of his father's business with a vision of a better life – a life in which he led a successful business with a team firing on all cylinders while he could watch his kids grow up. But this was the third time in a week that he was called back to work after hours to put out fires.

Sam had cast an aggressive vision for his team to double their revenue while maintaining their profit margins in the next five years so they could position themselves to sell. It would lead to a life-changing exit for everyone involved. But the business that was supposed to be a path to freedom had become a prison.

Although they were progressing toward the goal, Sam's effort was covering up the team's deficiencies. He was too involved in the weeds of the day-to-day operations and was spread too thin. The weight of the entire organization rested on his heroic efforts, and it wasn't sustainable. The scalability of the organization depended on the scalability of the team, but the team wasn't delivering.

They missed deadlines, took shortcuts, and spent more energy on petty politics than meeting objectives. Employees were firing emotional outbursts at each other in group messages, two of their top executives resented each other, and all the dysfunction had Sam worried he was about to lose his best team member. To make matters even more complicated, his brother was second in command and responsible for their next big product launch, but he was getting sloppy with the execution. Sam knew something had to change or else they would lose everything they had worked so hard for.

So he scheduled an off-site retreat for a come-to-Jesus-style meeting. Sam believed that if he confronted them with the reality of what was happening and inspired them with the potential they could accomplish, they would get their act together. To keep things from becoming too intense or dramatic, he mixed a bit of lightheared fun into the retreat. He hoped the combination would pay off. The future of the company depended on it.

At the end of the two-day event, it appeared the retreat was a success. The team heard the message and experienced an emotional high that galvanized the group. Everyone left motivated, energized, and believing in their future together. But six months later, everything they accomplished at the retreat appeared to have worn off.

One of the failing business units was still losing money, the key leader Sam was afraid to lose had left, and his replacement had upset their biggest client, causing his team to threaten to resign en masse. Relationships were deteriorating. Trust was eroding. It was clear nothing had changed. Sam was out of ideas.

With nowhere else to turn, Sam called his best friend and business mentor for help. His friend had just transferred ownership of his business to his son and was living the life he dreamed of. Sam wanted to know what he did to get there.

His friend told him that more intensity and effort wouldn't get him where he wanted to be. Taking the team on retreats, making motivational speeches, imposing threats, making new hires, or restructuring the org chart would all lead to short-term fixes that would eventually wear off. He told Sam that he was addressing the symptoms of the issues but missing what was actually causing the problems.

Sam believed his friend, but he wasn't sure what to do next. He had tried everything he knew, read, and had been trained to do, but none of it had worked, and he didn't know why.

His friend told him he didn't need more effort or intensity. He needed more clarity. "You're not seeing any progress because you can't see your blind spots," he told Sam.

Sam asked how he was supposed to see more clearly.

His friend said, "You need help. You need an experienced guide to help you see what's happening beneath the surface."

Sam told his friend that he was already working with a coach. His friend shook his head. "Your coach is giving you tools and advice, but he's not helping you change your mindset. He's not helping you see what you can't already see."

His friend suggested he call our team at SightShift™. We had helped Sam's friend prepare for his succession plan, and he was sure we could help Sam, too, so Sam called us.

We met Sam over a video chat to learn more about his business, the state of his team, and what they were trying to accomplish. During our call, we learned that Sam had everything we look for in a leader and business with great potential. He had an aggressive vision, an appreciation for operating systems, and, most importantly, he truly cared about the people on his team. Sam wasn't a bad leader. He was a good leader who was experiencing typical problems that every leader experiences and attempting to solve those problems the best way he knew how. Unfortunately, like many leaders, Sam had only been trained to solve these problems with new tools and more polished skills. He hadn't learned how to tap into the mindset necessary to transform the people. Without that transformation, he wasn't addressing the root cause of his team's issues. So, we laid out a vision of how we could help.

We put a plan in place to measure each member of his team to get a datatized view of the fixed and flexible parts of their mindset. The measurement would ensure he had the right people in the right spots and surface the blind spots that were sabotaging their effectiveness. Then, we would lead his team through a coaching process that would transform them into a high-functioning growth culture. After our conversation, Sam believed that more, better leaders would help them reach their financial goals, so he agreed to the plan, and we got to work.

After just one two-hour session with his team, the insights and vulnerability they expressed blew Sam away. Two weeks later, he called us excited about the progress they were already making. Everyone was budding with new awareness, and team meetings were slowly becoming more productive. Sam told us that no guest speaker, leadership book, or seminar had ever hit the depths we reached in such a short time.

I grinned at Sam and said, "We're just getting started. When we finish, they will thank you for the investment you made in them. Not just for the sake of the business, but because you will have changed their life."

Four years later, I stood with Sam in the living room of his new waterfront multi-million dollar home. He had just returned from his third once-in-a-lifetime vacation that year. He and his team had achieved their goal quicker than expected and experienced a life-changing exit with the sale of the company. More importantly, every individual on the leadership team was thriving; he left the business in better hands and was never called away from dinner with his family again.

As he reflected on the journey, Sam put his hand on my shoulder and said, "Thank you. I couldn't have gotten here without you."

I celebrated the achievement with him but couldn't take credit for his win. I didn't get him there. It was one idea, one choice, one path that we guided him and his organization to take.

If you are a leader, there are two paths you can take. You can lead for validation or you can lead for impact. The path of impact leads to joy, satisfaction, and healthy relationships. The path of validation leads to regret, resentment, and ruined relationships.

Most of the people in Sam's organization were leading and operating for their validation, which caused them to fall short of their potential. Unfortunately, this is happening in organizations of all sizes and every industry.

Too many leaders lead for validation, not impact. They lead to avoid their fears and alleviate their doubts. They lead for what they can *get* rather than what they can *give*.

Most don't do it intentionally; they do it reactively. They do it because they're stressed, feel pressure, or have lost focus. They do it for the results, out of self-preservation, or because they lack awareness.

When team leaders lead for validation, they develop other leaders who lead for validation, and it seeps into the entire organization. It becomes the culture. Executives obsess over appearances, micromanage team members, deflect accountability, and avoid addressing real issues. Employees respond by gossiping, engaging in office politics, undermining authority, and becoming complacent. It all results in a lot of wasted time, energy, and talent.

I've seen leaders from Fortune 100 companies to family-owned businesses fail to realize their potential, lose their direction, and ruin relationships because they never advance to leading for impact. I'm no exception.

I'm as guilty as anyone of leading for validation. Just ask my daughter whom I interrogated at Chick-fil-A on her third birthday about my worth as a dad. Or ask the employee I fired and his team that I lied to so I could save face. I've suffered my share of losses, big and small, at work and home. But my whole life changed when I learned to recognize when I am leading for validation and how to shift to leading for impact. And I want to help you do the same thing. That's why I started SightShift™.

SightShift™ is a leadership development company that utilizes a proprietary measurement tool and process to develop leaders who can see when they are leading for validation and can shift to leading for impact so that they can develop leaders who develop other leaders.

It's rare for people to reach the level of leadership where they are consistently leading for impact. Everyone from top-tier business consultants to adult development psychologists has conducted studies that show only about 2-3% of people ever reach the point they are leading for impact, not validation. But it is possible, you are capable, and SightShift™ can help you get there.

Who you become as a leader isn't determined by genetics; it doesn't have to be determined by your past experiences or upbringing. Neither nature nor nurture has to hinder you from becoming the leader you were meant to be. You just have to become aware of what's blocking you from becoming a leader of impact and learn how to transform those obstacles.

So many leaders fail to lead for impact because they have been poorly trained to be leaders – or not trained at all. Modern leadership development is shaped by cultural narratives and ideologies that might have good intentions but create soft, brittle leaders. They're not helping us become the kinds of leaders who develop leaders of impact.

One business called us asking for help. The company's operations had become slow and sloppy, and their annual engagement survey revealed they needed to rebuild trust within the organization. So, I laid out our process to measure the team members and lead them through a transformation process. The HR executive on the call responded, "We were hoping you could just put together some team-building exercises for a one-day event." She wanted trust falls, but needed transformation.

I understand not everyone is ready for total transformation up front, and I'm willing to meet potential clients where they are. So, I offered a two-hour event that would reveal with data exactly why they were experiencing their problems and introduce them to a leadership model that would transform their mindset.

Unfortunately, she was already convinced of the theatrics she needed to show her bosses a good-faith effort and not rock the boat with too much risk. So, we hung up the phone and didn't work together.

It's no wonder so many people prefer to work from home. In all my years of parenting and marriage, I have never once attempted to solve the thorniest relationship issues by putting my hand on their shoulder and offering to do a trust fall.

SightShift™ isn't in the business of surface-level quick fixes. We are in the business of life-changing transformation. If you want to become a leader who changes people's lives for the better, you'll have to go further than the popular leadership fads of our time. It will take more than gimmicky retreats, overpriced seminars, and motivational hacks. It will take more than mindfulness, empathy, and psychological safety. Leading for impact is not just a choice. It's a mindset that has to be developed. You will have to gain a deeper understanding of who you are, where you are, and where you are going.

This book aims to redefine what it means to be a world-class leader and provide a formula to get there. Ultimately, leaders who lead for validation are trying to get something externally that no one can give them. They're trying to get something that you can only find internally. When you find it, you will understand the essence of leadership, which can change people's lives for the better. You will lead for impact.

CHAPTER 2

THE IMPACT LEADER'S STRUGGLE™

Every leadership journey follows a similar progression. It begins with ambition. You want something or see something that could be bigger, better, or different. You have a vision for your company, team, or yourself to grow and advance.

You want to get a promotion or win an award. You want to double, triple, or even 10x your revenue. You want to move from number two in your category to number one. You want to add more locations to your franchise. You want to remove yourself from the day-to-day operations. You want to lead a successful exit or implement a smooth succession plan.

Some people have a combination of 17 different desires and struggle to stay focused each day. Others haven't discovered their vision yet, so their ambitious desire is frustrated and misguided.

One CEO we worked with struggled with the reality that he didn't desire to grow his organization. As he engaged in our process, he discovered that he didn't lack ambition. His vision was just dull. He found that he was searching for a deeper purpose and meaning. He didn't just want to build a business that made a lot of money. He wanted to build an organization that developed people.

Whatever the vision or desire, our ambition triggers our motivation to act. As we pursue our ambition, we experience struggle. This is normal on the leadership journey. If there's no struggle, there's no growth. The very fact that we want something means we have a vision bigger than the energy, time, skills, or resources that we currently have. There's a gap between where we are and where we want to be. The struggle to close this gap induces pressure.

Externally, we feel pressure to choose the right direction, make the right decisions, deliver on promises, hit the target, or secure our future. Eventually, the external pressure becomes internal pressure. We interpret the potential outcomes of the external challenge as an indictment of who we are. When external pressure seeps into the core of who we are, it causes us to feel doubts.

You made big promises, but now you wonder if you can deliver. "What will they think of me if I don't come through?"

You know you can lead a company of $30 million in revenue, but you wonder if you have what it takes to lead a company at $100 million. "What will it say about me if I can't?"

You're leading the team in a new strategic direction to exploit market opportunities, but what if it goes wrong? "If we lose our way, will I lose my hold on this organization?"

You want to grow your team so you can be less involved in the day-to-day and expand the company, but what will happen if they can't carry the weight? "Will I have to step in and rescue them again?"

You want to hand over the company to a family member, but you wonder if they have what it takes. "What will happen to our relationship if they fail? What will happen to my retirement income? Will I resent them?"

These internal doubts expose flaws in our mindset and reveal our insecurity. It becomes an inflection point. How we respond in these insecure moments will determine our path. It will determine whether we can sustain the endurance necessary to finish the race or if we lose our motivation to see the vision become a reality. It will determine whether we can stay calm when things don't go as we expect them to or if we lose our minds during chaos. It will determine whether we change lives or ruin relationships. It will determine whether we lead for impact or lead for validation.

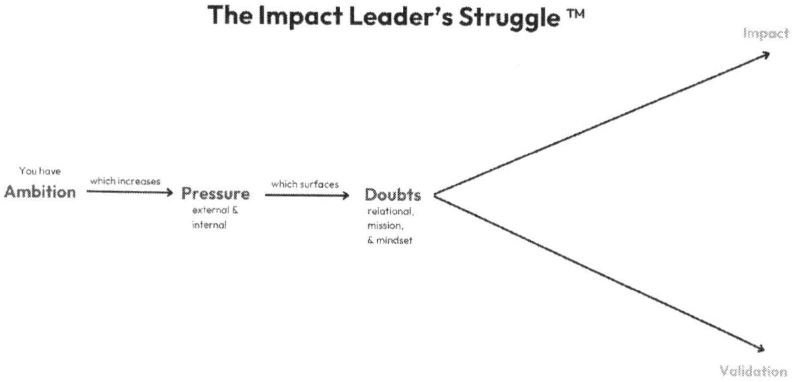

Leaders who lead for impact have a vision they are willing to sacrifice for, can stay calm during chaos, and care for those they lead. As the pressure builds and the doubts set in, we drift towards leading for validation. When we start leading for validation, our sacrifice turns to dread, our calm turns to anger, and our caring turns to bitterness.

Sacrifice to Dread

At the beginning of any leadership journey, we set out to be as good a leader as possible and are willing to pay the price to see our vision become a reality. But over time, as the demands intensify or we progress to a new vision, we begin to dread the sacrifices required for our role.

Years ago, I moved my young family back to my wife's home state to take a leadership position where I was responsible for turning around a failing organization. It was a challenging journey. Things got worse before they got better. I endured backlash from the team for my decisions and had to take a significant pay cut to keep the organization afloat. After years of effort and failure, the organization finally experienced a rebirth. It was a sweet victory, but I gave so much to achieve it. With a new leadership team in place and things operating smoothly, I felt the freedom to skip a team bonding function. In my mind, I had earned the right to stay home with my family because of my years of sacrifice to the team and the organization. But the team didn't feel the same way. To say it upset them is an understatement. I had a small mutiny on my hands.

In the turmoil, my mind flashed back six months earlier. I remembered walking into a meeting thinking, "I don't care if I ever lead another one of these meetings again." It was a subtle, fleeting thought, but it was the first sign that I was beginning to dread the sacrifice required to lead this team and take it to the next level. Their minor mutiny was connected to a major insight hidden in my heart.

Rather than pay attention to that feeling, I let it pass and kept going through the motions. My heart wasn't fully in it anymore; eventually, it caught up to me. The team lost confidence in me, our trust eroded, and I became angry. I felt stuck and frozen physically and emotionally. I remember going for a run and screaming out loud at the top of my lungs. I had a minor breakdown. For the first time, I couldn't show up and perform in my role. I was at a loss of meaning for what I was doing.

When so much of our meaning is wrapped in what we do, and dread starts to occur, we deteriorate from within. Some leaders experience it in small ways with mini breakdowns. For others, it turns into a major breakdown. Some leaders experience physical breakdowns. Others experience mental and emotional breakdowns. We've worked with leaders who went on auto-pilot, losing key talent and missing significant opportunities while they tried to recover. Others disappeared for two years and used an assistant or family member to run the company while everyone wondered why the boss wasn't more involved. One leader sold his company looking for relief only to find tighter handcuffs in the new situation.

Our emotional connection to the mission drives the meaning we make from what we are doing. When the emotional connection changes, it can initiate the slow drift toward leading for validation. Rather than pay attention to what's happening, most leaders prop themselves up with hype or substances to keep going or settle for the most popular form of relief, a vacation. They expect to return refreshed, renewed, and motivated again but usually discover the internal pressure traveled with them. So, instead, they power through until some arbitrary finish line when they can finally relax. Unfortunately, that finish line never arrives.

We don't need more hype, stimulants, or a vacation to get us back on the path of impact. We need a new horizon. We need to remember who we are and why we are doing what we are doing. It may be time to leave our current role or we may need to make new meaning out of what we are currently doing. The vision we pursue doesn't care how much we've sacrificed up to this point. If we build the horizon we pursue around our validation, we will experience the next emotion: anger.

Calm to Angry

As we slide from sacrifice to dread and lose the meaning of our work, our need for validation reveals itself in anger. We become frustrated with our circumstances, or with poor execution, or with missed assignments, or lack of initiative, or lost opportunities. In our frustration, we lose sight of the true direction we need to take. Eventually, we take that frustration out on the people, but you can't lead anyone well when you're frustrated with them, including yourself.

In May 2022, the CEO of one of the world's largest furniture companies held an all-employee meeting to discuss the state of their business. At the end of the meeting she went on a tirade admonishing employees for being more concerned about not receiving their bonuses than they were about hitting the company's $26 million revenue target.

"Don't ask about, 'What are we going to do if we don't get a bonus?' Get the damn $26 million," she said. "Spend your time and your effort thinking about the $26 million we need and not thinking about what are you going to do if we don't get a bonus, all right?"

Meanwhile, she received a multi-million dollar bonus from the company on top of her seven-figure salary.

To make the matter worse, the meeting was recorded on Zoom. Her rant was posted on social media and the clip went viral. Nearly 8 million people saw her outburst.

It's possible that she is an emotionally aware, intelligent, and composed leader under normal circumstances. But in this particular season of the company, she was likely moving toward dread, and under stress, it revealed itself in anger. Because she couldn't properly order the stress in her mind, an 80-second clip of a 75-minute meeting sabotaged so much of her leadership capacity with that team.

She did write an apology to the employees afterward, but it will take many more positive moments of leadership to overcome this one moment of insecurity.

The drift toward leading for validation starts with a few angry outbursts that chip away at our authority and credibility. Then, it turns into many angry outbursts that create an environment of fear. Before long, we've completely diminished our ability to impact the team. We wonder why we can't get things to work and why we can't build a high-functioning team to solve the problems. We get frustrated because we have to step in and rescue them again, only to step away and see it all fall apart again.

Publicly we may apologize for the outbursts because we don't want to lose the team, but privately, we start to blame our shortcomings on the people. When we reach this point, we have a choice to make. We can get angry, or we can build a better system to develop leaders. Most choose the easy path of anger, which causes our relationships to fracture.

Caring to Bitter

After the dread turns to anger and we become frustrated with the people we are leading, our care for them turns to bitterness. We get sick of being around them. We question why we brought them onto the team in the first place. We believe they don't appreciate what we're doing for them. Next thing you know, co-founders can't get along anymore, family members become divided, partners who were like sisters no longer see eye-to-eye, or an otherwise talented team fractures. If we're unaware of the slide toward leading for validation, the journey will end with broken relationships.

A multi-location franchise that we worked with experienced this drift. The dad, who was the founder and owner of the business, had reached the edge of his current leadership potential. Rather than investing in his growth, he leaned on old tactics of manipulation and pressure to control his team. Everyone on the team began to dread working there. To make matters worse, his team included his wife, son, daughter, and son-in-law. They all complained about his outbursts and threatened to leave, including his spouse! Despite their pleas for him to get help, he wasn't ready to embrace the change necessary to grow. His resistance led the family to become bitter. Eventually, the son left, the family fractured, and the business suffered. We see this all too often when leaders fail to invest in their own growth.

Unfortunately, most people don't notice they're leading for validation until the bitterness sets in. They ignore the dread and they apologize for the anger, but they never lean in and explore what's causing these emotions. The next thing they know, relationships are broken beyond repair and they are left with resentment and regret.

These moments that trigger our insecurities test our leadership constantly and pressure us to lead for validation. How we respond in these moments can make or break our success. It's our insecure moments that ruin our leadership. To become aware of when your insecurity negatively impacts your leadership so you can pass this test, use the SightShift Validation Check™.

The SightShift Validation Check™

The SightShift Validation Check™ is a tool designed to help us notice when we are drifting toward the path of leading for validation. It consists of three scales.

The first scale measures when your sacrifice is becoming dread. The second scale measures where your calm demeanor is turning to anger. The third scale measures when you drift from caring to bitter in your relationships.

At any point on our leadership journey, we can take one, two, or all three of these scales and diagnose our current state. It's not a perfect science, but if we are honest with our assessment, we can start to notice when we are drifting toward leading for validation. It can become a signal that we are no longer leading for impact, and we can check ourselves before we wreck ourselves.

SightShift Validation Check™

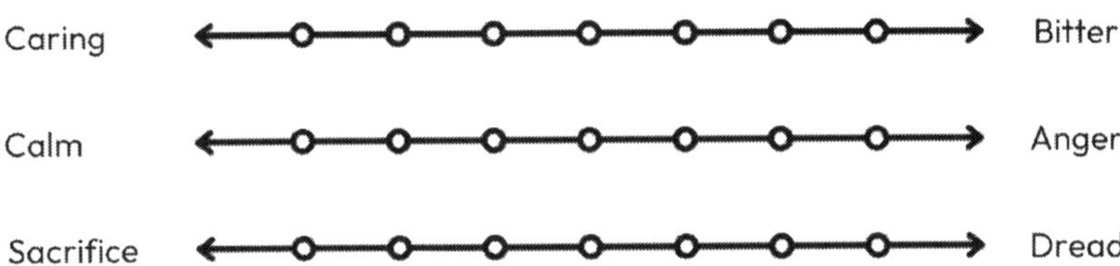

Great leaders are willing to pay the price for a vision, can stay calm under pressure, and maintain a heart for people despite the challenges. The challenge for everyone who wants to be a great leader and lead for impact is to learn how their insecurity shapes their leadership.

CHAPTER 3

ALL LEADERS FACE INSECURITY

No one wakes up wanting to lead from dread, anger, and bitterness, yet it happens to so many people. This slide toward leading for validation happens because we are insecure. Whether you realize it or not, insecurity is shaping your decisions, your reactions, your motivation, and the environment you are creating. It doesn't matter if you are just beginning or have years of experience. Everyone who is on a leadership journey has moments of insecurity.

I have over 25 years of leadership experience, and I still have moments when I am insecure as a leader. I have moments when I want more power, moments when I want to win no matter what it takes, and moments when I lie to make myself sound better than I am. I have moments when I want to quit. I have moments where I wonder if it's worth it. We have these moments because we want people to think we are doing a good job and want them to like us. We are not aware that the driving energy in most of our leadership is an insecurity we seek to comfort.

Who we become as leaders and who the people we lead become hinges on how we respond in our moments of insecurity. We become a better or worse version of who we are, and the people we lead become better or worse because of our leadership. If we can open our eyes to our insecurities and how they influence our leadership, we can transform them into powerful moments of impact.

This is what SightShift™ helps leaders do. We help leaders transform their insecurities to become leaders of impact who develop other leaders of impact.

We have worked with leaders from all over the world, in various industries, and at every level of experience. For all of them, the path to impact is the same. It's a journey of self-mastery and discovery of who you are, where you are, and why you're here. This journey begins with becoming increasingly aware of your insecurity.

When we work with people trying to improve from novice to pro as leaders, it's relatively easy to make that improvement. All they need is a few reflective moments when they become aware of how their insecurity shows up. If you've read my other books or experienced any of our programs, you know we have many stories of people surfacing this awareness. Whether it happens in their personal or professional lives, our favorite stories are the small moments when someone shifts from the path of validation to impact. Like one CEO who realized he could apologize rather than argue his way into being right. Or like the business owner who realized he didn't have to ride his father's coattails but could pursue his own ambition. Or like when I realized I was leading team meetings like a loaded gun, cocked and ready to shoot down any protest to protect my credibility and authority.

One client lit up my phone with excited texts. He had just made the most significant pitch in the history of his marketing agency and won the deal. He said, "It worked! I used what I learned from working with you to go into the meeting, be myself and strategic, and win the deal!" He was already on the path of progress before we met, but what he learned working with us was how to make an even more significant impact by being aware of his insecurities. He was now on the path to becoming world-class.

Growth becomes more challenging for leaders trying to move beyond pro and become world-class. In these cases, growth comes from learning how their insecurity subtly chips away at their effectiveness. Like the Fortune 100 president we worked with, who realized that her lack of vulnerability kept the people she led at a distance. She was trying to protect her power and control, but it kept everyone on edge. People were unsure about their status in the organization and felt disconnected from the core mission.

Once she became aware of this, she changed how she addressed the organization. When she prepared to present to the board, she didn't prepare to impress them out of her need for validation. She prepared to impact them. When she addressed her team, she openly shared her doubts and weaknesses to help them feel more connected to her. As a result, the team became more engaged with the vision. Eventually, they became so effective that she shut off her phone and took a month-long vacation with her family for the first time in her career.

It's more challenging to improve from pro to world-class because we have created an environment where we don't notice our insecurities. Society has encouraged us to stuff them down, ignore them, or fight against them. It has labeled them the enemy of success, but that's not helping us grow.

If we consider our insecurities an enemy to our growth, our brains will trigger us to fight against them. But that's not how transformation works. You don't transform by fighting insecurities, shaming them, or starving them. If you do that long enough, they will form a coup inside you and cause all kinds of destruction. You transform insecurity by paying attention to it, welcoming it to the table, and feeding it better food. Our insecurities are not something to resist. They are a clue to what's developing in us and a signal to where we can grow.

As we grow and develop, we will have fewer and fewer of these moments, but we still have them. All leaders do. But the more we pay attention to them, learn from them, and transform them, the more confident we become as leaders.

The source of true confidence

Every leader desires to be the kind of person who can walk into a room with confidence. The kind of leader who can communicate a vision, guide a team through transition, and set standards with authority. We struggle to be this kind of leader because of our insecurities. Our insecurities cause us to show up too big or too small in our most important leadership moments.

Some leaders over-project confidence. They hype themselves with power poses and grand gestures. They overplay one attribute or character trait that projects their strength. They draw authority from their title rather than their vision, clarity, and understanding. They believe you must be overly assertive, bordering on being a jerk to get things done. This fake confidence is fueled by insecurity and usually comes across as arrogance. Ultimately, it sabotages their impact.

Other leaders swing to the opposite extreme. They don't want to come across as arrogant or pushy, so they hold back. They succumb to their doubts and hide from their best selves. They avoid taking risks, shy away from challenging situations, defer to others, and fail to assert their most valuable strengths. As a result, they diminish themselves and their impact.

Both approaches are attempts to avoid our insecurities and control others' perceptions of us. They are responses to the doubts we have about who we are. Even the best leaders are not 100% confident all the time. We all experience doubt. However, a genuinely confident leader has assurance about them even in doubt. They aren't full of hype, nor do they suppress their brilliance. They have nothing to prove and nothing to hide. They inspire people with their wins and relax them by sharing their struggles. They tear down the pedestals people place them on and can laugh at their insecurities. As a result, they build a healthy, thriving environment where everyone feels seen, known, and heard.

True confidence comes from knowing who you are, where you are, and why you're here.

A leader with this kind of confidence leads for impact, not validation. But you can only develop this confidence after you experience an identity shift.

CHAPTER 4
INSTITUTIONS ARE FAILING US

So many leaders struggle with insecurity because we haven't experienced an identity shift. We don't know who we are, what we are to do, or where we can have an impact. As a result, we are building our lives around emptiness in search of meaning. We can trace this emptiness to a failure of our institutions.

Institutions used to guide individuals through an identity shift. Whether it was the tribe, the government, the church, the family, or a business, they would use rituals to aid young people in the process of becoming. Through these rituals, people discovered who they are and what they are to do. The institutions helped people make meaning for themselves and provided the context of a community where they could express their impact.

Take, for example, the ritual some Native American tribes used to acknowledge the transition of boys becoming men. Boys would retreat to a sacred site in nature chosen by the elders and fast for four days and four nights. During this time, the boy would pray for a vision to help him find his purpose and role in the community. After receiving the vision, the elders would help the boy interpret it and certify his passage into adulthood. There was a before-and-after experience where the boy received a new identity, and the community affirmed it. There was an awakening, a revelation, and a commitment to a purpose.

The Ojibwe tribe conducts a similar coming-of-age ritual for girls that begins at the start of their first menstruation. Girls will fast from specific foods for an entire year and seclude themselves from family and community interactions during menstruation each month. They use this time to focus on personal growth and learn from their elders. At the end of the year, the entire community celebrates her transition into womanhood with a feast. Following the ritual, the new woman still experiences hormonal changes. She still struggles with typical questions that come with growing up, but the ritual provides a clearly defined transition and identity shift. It gives her identity, purpose, and relationship.

Other tribes and communities conduct similar rituals. Jewish boys experience a bar mitzvah at 13, ritualizing their transition into adulthood and affirming their participation in religious activities. Latin American girls experience a quinceanera on their 15th birthday, celebrating their transition from childhood to adulthood.

In all these examples, when done effectively, the institution uses rituals to guide the individual through a transformation of becoming and cement their identity shift. They make it clear: this is who you are, where you are, and why you're here. But most of society doesn't experience this anymore.

Most of our rituals have become hollow. They've become reenactments to preserve cultural traditions or shallow excuses to party. The most meaningful rituals most people experience today are school graduations. Unfortunately, passing a standardized test doesn't prepare you for the world or result in an identity shift.

We now have entire generations of people progressing through life and entering the workforce lost. They lack confidence, purpose, and direction. They are searching for meaning and community. They are asking, "Who am I? What am I to do? Where do I belong?"

The Baby Boomer generation looked for meaning in their work and built their identity around their careers. Their sense of meaning and self-worth rose and fell with the success and failure of their jobs.

Millennials and Gen Z have rejected that. They don't want to be defined by their work or career. They're growing up connected to a thousand different societies and a thousand different ways to build an identity. As a result, they build their identity around a patchwork of pieces. They take the least validated part of who they are, whether it's their race, gender, sexuality, or creed, and magnify it to make it *all* of who they are. But that's not enough to hold up their whole identity either. We are more than any one marker and more than our roles or relationships.

Since our institutions don't guide people through an identity shift or help individuals make their own meaning anymore, we become entrapped by their agenda. We attach ourselves to political parties, ideological movements, and conspiracy theories to tell us who to be, what to believe, and how to behave so we can belong. Whoever controls the algorithm controls our mind.

These institutions aren't helping us become better versions of ourselves. They are led by insecure leaders who lead for validation, not impact. They believe people exist to serve the institution rather than the institution existing to serve the people. They've hijacked our meaning, and, as a result, they are developing people who lead for validation at an even grander scale.

Company leaders are starting to adjust to this new reality by investing in the people on their team, but they aren't going far enough. They're completing HR checkboxes without addressing core needs for transformation that truly develop leaders of impact. They invest in overpriced seminars and gimmicky retreats that trumpet the latest leadership fads. They install ping pong tables in the office and arrange bowling outings for team bonding. They promote mindfulness as the antidote to stress but don't address the root cause of the stress. They prioritize empathy as a way to connect but don't offer tangible ways to solve problems. They create psychologically safe environments but remove the very thing that helps us grow. Our new rituals involve trust falls and ropes courses. Modern leadership development practices aren't answering our biggest problem.

The point here isn't to burn down institutions. The point is to transform them. A healthy institution exists to serve the people. It exists to assist the process of becoming. It exists to help the individual make their own meaning and become the best version of themselves. This approach doesn't mean institutions should focus solely on the individual at the expense of the collective. Healthy teams consist of healthy individuals. If the institution helps develop healthy individuals, it will benefit the collective. To do this, the institution needs healthy leaders leading the way.

If you lead a team, an organization, or a family, you represent the institution. With that comes a responsibility. The people on your team likely haven't experienced an identity shift. They are searching for meaning and a guide to help them navigate who they are becoming. You can be that guide, but it will require a different leadership approach from what we've been trained in. You can't just force the organization's values and beliefs onto them and conform them to your identity for your purpose. Instead, you will have to help them discover who they are and their unique impact on the mission. You will have to teach them how to recognize when they are leading for validation and how to become leaders of impact so they can actively participate in building a healthy environment. To help them become leaders of impact, *you* must lead for impact first.

CHAPTER 5

THE FORMULA FOR IMPACT

One of the problems with leadership and leadership development is that there's no clear definition of great leadership that we all agree on, and there are no standard metrics to measure whether someone is developing as a leader. It's not like finances, which have uniform language, metrics, and formulas to tell us exactly what's happening, where we're going, and how we get there. Even in companies that use tools like adjusted EBITDA to influence the story, there are core fundamentals that guide the process of financial modeling that leadership modeling lacks.

Because there are no clear fundamentals or definitions of great leadership, most leaders settle for trying to appease the people they lead. We measure our effectiveness with subjective questions like, "Am I doing a good job?" and "Do they like me?"

This approach to evaluating and developing leaders results in a team of executives who are over-promoted doers. They advance to the C-suite because the right people generally like them and they get stuff done, but they haven't developed into leaders of impact who can develop other leaders. As a result, most of them drift towards leading for validation and to please whoever they care about. But it's impossible to please everyone.

The essence of leadership is you will take people somewhere they have never been before, somewhere they haven't even imagined or thought of yet. The new horizon will disrupt their status quo. The ambitious pursuit will raise the standards and demand more from them. This change and uncertainty will draw out their insecurities. Some will hide. Some will become aggressive. Some will try to over-protect and resist change. Some will be flooded with doubt and wonder if it's even possible to get where you're leading them. If you're unaware of how their insecurities will be triggered or unequipped to lead them through change, their resistance will draw out your insecurities. It will create an environment where everyone is proving and hiding rather than marching together toward a shared goal.

One organization we worked with had an ambitious vision to grow and sell the company, but they knew they couldn't get there without investing in their leaders, so they called us to help. As we began defining great leadership and coaching their team to this standard, one executive displayed unusual behavior that alerted my spidey senses. She was irrationally distant and confusing and tried to cover it up with smiles and laughs. Calling her behavior weird is an understatement. It concerned me so much that I met with the CEO about it. That particular department was already falling short of the organization's standards, and I had a hunch that it could be even worse than expected. Without revealing confidential information from our coaching conversations, I advised the CEO to pay closer attention. When he examined the situation more carefully, he found 18 months of unreconciled financial information within their international accounts.

At some point, the pursuit of their vision outpaced this leader's capacity and character. It took her out of her depth. Rather than being transformed by the insecurity, she let the insecurity dictate her actions. She chose to hide rather than ask for help (and this was a healthy organization where most people felt comfortable asking for help). The messy financials were wrecking the company's ability to forecast, plan, and ultimately position themselves for a sale. Without a defined standard for great leadership, the destruction her insecurities were causing could have wrecked a life-changing deal. This is why developing healthy leaders is so crucial.

An organization without leaders who lead for impact will get in their own way and sabotage their own efforts. But without a defined process or target for developing leaders, how do you know if you're getting it done? How do you know how to lead for impact?

The Formula for Impact

Impact is your effect on a person or a community of people. It can be the people in your family, team, organization, or clients you serve. When you impact someone, you change their life.

Ultimately, we express our impact as leaders through what we value. When we are insecure and leading for validation, our values get out of balance. We over- and undervalue elements of leadership and express our values in extremes. The value itself isn't good or bad. It's the expression of the value that distorts our impact. It's like plucking a guitar string to create a beautiful melody. A healthy value is expressed in the tension points of its extremes.

For example, you might value engagement as a leader. You want to be enthusiastic about the mission and you want everyone else to be enthusiastic with you. Your energy and excitement will have a powerful impact on the people you lead, but if you're unaware of how your insecurity shapes this value, it can get out of balance and diminish your impact. You can overvalue the parts of the mission that stimulate and excite you and undervalue the parts that require stillness and thoughtful reflection. If you value engagement, the strength of your leadership will be your pursuit of the next idea. A weakness of your leadership will be not sitting with an idea long enough to understand it before you take action. Both approaches are needed. How you apply this value will shape how you impact the people you lead and your team's success.

Take another example. You might value achievement and getting things done, which is important for successful leaders. But if you're unaware of the insecurity that drives your ambition, you may overvalue winning to the point that you push too hard and burn yourself and others out. And you might undervalue incremental progress even if it doesn't meet specific benchmarks. If you value achievement, the strength of your leadership will be getting your team across the finish line and accomplishing big goals. The weakness of your leadership will be not genuinely celebrating progress to keep your team motivated.

In another case, you may value strength and power in leadership. If you are unaware of how your insecurity shapes this value, you will overvalue protecting power and undervalue empowering others. The insecure part of you will try to amass tons of power because you have something to prove, or it will disguise your hunger for power because you feel shame about your desire. As a result, you will hide from the true strength of who you are. When you lead for impact, you won't hide from your desire for power or consolidate power for your interest. You will grow your power to give it away and multiply it. This approach represents the true essence of leading for impact.

When you lead for impact, you won't seek to get what *you* value. Instead, you will *give* what other people value. Insecure leaders get so wrapped up in what they value they can't appreciate the values of others. Instead, they just become virtue signalers. They become so focused on signaling to the world what is important to them that they can't see the full human experience of anyone else. Their values get out of balance. They lead for validation.

One team we worked with had a CMO who crossed his arms during our coaching session and said defiantly, "I don't have any insecurities." During one of our breaks, I noticed him bragging about the people who came to his house for a weekend party. He pulled out his phone and forced a photo show on an uninterested audience. He couldn't see his insecurity, but everyone else could.

He valued belonging. Driven by his insecurity, he was proving that he belonged by bragging about the status of his house guests. At the same time, he was utterly inept at building belonging on his team. He kept everyone at arm's distance, and no one ever knew where they stood with him. If he could acknowledge his insecurity and transform it, he could be great at making his team feel like they belonged. Unfortunately, he couldn't get past his defenses to admit he was insecure. Instead, the rest of the organization grew past his insecurity, and six months later, he was no longer on the team.

Secure leaders can balance their values and lead for impact rather than validation. World-class leaders take this one step further. They balance the entire team's values to create a healthy, thriving environment.

On a truly diverse team, everyone values something different about leadership. We reveal what we value through our stories, complaints, frustrations, and ideas. However, most people don't realize that their values are shaped by their unique wiring, and their past experiences and insecurities shape their concern for those values.

When we lead for validation, we lead the team like a thermometer. Out of our insecurity, we either reflect our values at extremes or try to reflect what someone else wants in their insecurity. As a result, our values get out of balance, and our team's values get out of balance.

When we are secure in who we are and leading for impact, we lead the team like a thermostat. We don't just give what makes us feel good or appeases the people. We tune the dial of values up or down based on the environment's needs.

There is no single value that makes a great leader or team. A great leader appreciates the values of everyone on the team and can keep those values in balance. This is easier said than done.

To keep our values in balance, we must stay vigilant about our actions and be aware of our motives. The SightShift Impact Formula™ helps us do that.

The SightShift Impact Formula™

Impact = Right Action + Right Motive

Our impact is determined by the sum of our actions and the motives that shape those actions. We diminish our impact when we take the wrong action at the wrong time or with the wrong motive.

For instance, you may value logical thinking. On the surface, it sounds like a wise approach to leadership, but when you're leading for validation, you can take the wrong action at the wrong time. You may wait too long for the data to confirm the direction and miss the necessary risk that your intuition suggests. When you lead for impact, you take the right action at the right time.

That doesn't mean the right action is always the opposite of what you value. The right action right now might be to be patient and look at the data more. It might be to take the intuitive leap before calculating all the data. The challenge and art of great leadership is being aware of what you value and being able to discern between actions that lead to impact and actions that come from your need for validation. You can tell the difference by paying attention to your motives.

Motive is the impulse that causes us to act. It's our motivation. It comes from our deepest desire, which we want more than anything else. When we are stressed or overwhelmed, our doubts shape our motives.

Every leader has doubts. We doubt if we are capable, if we're doing enough, if we belong, if we are needed, if we're prepared enough, if they believe in us, if we're being heard. Our brains convince us these doubts are true, but they aren't. If we look closer, these doubts reveal our insecurity about who we are.

One night, our team had a meeting scheduled to close a deal with a large multinational company. It was a tremendous opportunity to impact a successful company by helping them develop their leaders. Because of the time zone difference, we had to schedule the meeting at 8 p.m. my time. I no longer had an office at my house, so I used my daughter's bedroom for the meeting while she was at work. I made her bed to prepare for the meeting because it was in the camera's background.

The meeting went great, and we closed the deal. I sat in the living room, reveling in the success when my daughter came home. She walked up to her room, saw the bed made, and texted me: "Dad, you can use my room, just ask next time."

Keep in mind, this is a room in the house that *I pay for*, with an electric bill that *I pay for*, with a water bill that *I pay for*, with a trash service that *I pay for*. I could feel the energy pulsing through my legs as I read her text. I wanted to text back: "YOUR room? Oh thank you for the privilege of using YOUR room!"

At that moment, the thing I wanted most was validation of my doubts. Closing the deal made me feel worthy, but my daughter wasn't participating in my parade. I wanted her to celebrate my work to close the deal so she could have a warm, comfortable place to sleep at night. I wanted her to express gratitude and affirm that I was an awesome dad and provider. I wanted her to think so highly of me that she would be happy for me to use her room whenever I wanted.

Any calm, rational person would notice that she wasn't diminishing my worth. She was setting appropriate boundaries. It was my insecurity that interpreted it as a threat.

Thankfully, I didn't send the text. Without awareness of the insecurity driving my behavior, I would have incited an unnecessary power struggle that could have damaged our relationship. I would have failed to appreciate that she felt ownership over a space and took care of it. I would have missed what was most pure and true about my daughter and our relationship: that she is a grateful, responsible, ambitious person, and I'm so glad I get to be her dad. Thankfully, I didn't make that moment about my validation.

Under stress or pressure, the thing we want most is validation for our doubts. It's what causes us to act too aggressively or too passively or to ruminate endlessly and not act at all. The insecurity we feel stimulates our brains and triggers us to act. You will know your doubts drive you when you notice your values are out of balance.

Take, for example, the value of boundaries. Most people will agree that healthy boundaries are important to building a healthy team. However, when we lead for validation, our fears and insecurity distort our motives and skew our actions.

If you fear vulnerability because you've been taken advantage of in the past, you will create boundaries that are too rigid. You will take action to keep everyone at arm's distance so no one can hurt you again. Because you act from insecure motives, you will cut off opportunities to build genuine connections.

If you doubt that you are needed, you will create boundaries that are too permeable. You will say yes to everything and everyone to ensure you are a part of the process. Because you act out of insecure motives, you will create an environment of co-dependent relationships that don't allow individual autonomy.

If you doubt whether or not you are good enough, you won't care about boundaries at all as long as you win. The end result will help alleviate your doubt, but everyone else will feel abused and neglected along the way.

Each of these approaches to boundaries is an example of how our insecurity ruins our leadership. They all value the same thing, boundaries, but are shaped by different insecurities, which leads to the wrong action taken with the wrong motive. This disparity is why leadership development has been challenging to quantify, track, and measure. Everyone sees leadership differently, and different insecurities shape everyone.

When we evaluate leadership through the SightShift Impact Formula™, we can quantify and measure leaders' growth and development. We can assess our actions and the motives behind them. We can become aware of when we take action for our comfort and when we take action to impact others. We can pinpoint the insecurity that keeps us from becoming the leaders we were meant to be. With this awareness, there is no ceiling on the impact we can have.

Unfortunately, modern leadership development is distorting the formula for impact. We're told mindfulness is the key to dealing with our stress and insecurity, but we're not learning how to upgrade our mindset to transform our insecurity into impact. We're told we need empathy for the whole world, but we're not taking action to end anyone's suffering. We're told we have to create psychologically safe environments to protect people from the doubts they feel, but we're lowering the demands of excellence.

Mindfulness, empathy, and psychological safety alone don't make great leaders. They are good starting points but terrible ending points. They fall short of developing leaders who develop other leaders of impact. If you want to become a leader of impact, you will have to experience a mindset upgrade, you will have to discover your mercy-based mission, and you will have to create an environment that raises the standard, not lowers it.

The SightShift Impact Formula™

Impact = Right Action + Right Motive

The Ancient Formula

Justice = Mercy + Humility

The Broken Formula

Mindfulness = Empathy + Psychological Safety

PART 2

WHY MINDFULNESS, EMPATHY, AND PSYCHOLOGICAL SAFETY DON'T MAKE GREAT LEADERS

CHAPTER 6

MONKS DON'T BUILD GREAT TEAMS

The first way modern leadership development distorts the SightShift Impact Formula™ is by emphasizing mindfulness as the key to dealing with our stress and insecurity.

Most leaders today fail to have an impact because we don't lead with awareness. We become so connected to our circumstances and consumed by stress and pressure that we aren't aware of how our insecurity causes our values to get out of balance. Because we can't see clearly, we lead mindlessly. We unknowingly allow our insecurities to drive our attention, direction, and action. We get distracted by worries about the future or regrets about the past. We fight against reality and our current circumstances and comfort our doubts by doubling down on what we overvalue. This wasted activity compounds our stress, depleting our effectiveness, decaying our relationships, and destroying our lives. As a response, leaders turn to mindfulness for relief.

Mindfulness moves us into the driver's seat of our attention. It helps us focus on the present moment. It allows us to momentarily separate ourselves from the circumstances that trigger our insecurity so we can process what is happening to us, in us, and around us. It puts a pause between the stress we feel and our reaction to that stress. It puts us in a state where we can observe our thoughts, feelings, and emotions so they don't dominate us, and we don't have to stuff them down and ignore them. It allows us to unload our burdens and accept reality as it is. This increased awareness is an essential step in having an impact through our leadership, but we can't stop there. Just "being present" doesn't change the world. "Being present" is the approach for monks.

Monks are great models for the power of mindfulness meditation, but the shortcoming of their approach is they never move beyond mindfulness. They may master self-reliance and individual growth, but they don't build great teams. They may find enlightenment, but they don't impact communities. They may come to peace with the world's injustices, but they don't seek justice in the world. This way of life moves some people, but I'm more inspired by those who experience a meditation practice so profoundly that it moves them to act. They start a business or a family that impacts the world and their community. They get up off the mat and change lives.

In my experience, the people who do the most yoga and meditation retreats tend to have the most fragile and selfish demeanors. One organization that contacted us was experiencing disgraceful moral failures among their C-suite executives. To navigate the turmoil, the CEO leaned on a coach who helped him feel at peace, even enlightened, despite the abysmal results. Every executive worked with a coach 1-on-1, but no one was honest about the fact that the team wasn't achieving results. The point of coaching and reflection isn't just to feel OK with your current circumstances or have a place to vent. The point is to be able to accept reality and then do something about it.

Leaders who lead for impact know how to be present *and* engaged. They know how to leverage circumstances to grow other leaders. Mindfulness alone doesn't make us leaders of impact. We have to translate our awareness into meaningful action. Getting stuck in the monk phase of endless meditation means you're not getting something you need. I've experienced meditation practices that had me staring at the wall for hours until I felt all my ambition evaporate. Instructors said I would find contentment here, but this is not contentment. The state I reached created an emptiness that needed to be filled with something more powerful. It was a state that needed the benefit of a mindset upgrade. When you stop at mindfulness, you're not experiencing the transformation of a mindset upgrade that makes mindfulness valuable.

A mindset upgrade occurs in the quiet space of mindfulness. This upgrade fills us with the truth of who we are. The doubt we feel about who we are is proven untrue, and we become secure in our identity. We get what we need internally rather than externally through our actions. As a result, we can discern the right action to take and assess the purity of our motives. The purpose of this isn't just naval-gazing. The purpose is to purify our motives. The pure in heart will see more than everyone else. The more we see, the more we won't be driven by our insecurity or the need for validation, which sets us up to lead for impact.

When we lead mindlessly, we are unaware, distracted, and fighting against reality. When we lead with mindfulness, we become aware, present, and accept reality. When we experience a mindset upgrade, we become aware and proactive and transform reality. It sets us up to have an impact.

You can think of it like driving a car. Leading mindlessly is like driving a car on autopilot. We go through the motions without awareness and with little engagement. We react to stimuli without conscious intention or direction.

Leading with mindfulness is like driving the car with full attention and presence. We are aware of every turn of the wheel, every press of the pedal, and every vehicle around us. We make deliberate choices, respond calmly to challenges, and appreciate the journey, not just the destination.

When we experience a mindset upgrade, we lead like skilled race car drivers. We are strategic and proactive. We anticipate obstacles, plan our route meticulously, and constantly refine our skills. We don't just navigate the road; we master it.

Experiencing mindfulness without a mindset upgrade is like making a pit stop without changing the tires. Eventually, the car will wobble again.

If we try to re-engage our circumstances without a mindset upgrade, our insecurities will fill us again. Our subconscious will trigger us to comfort our doubts and protect our insecurity. We will return to taking action for our validation.

Experiencing a mindset upgrade doesn't mean we will never face insecurity again. As long as we are growing, we will always face moments of insecurity. The goal is to face them in new challenges and on new race tracks that can help us learn more about who we are. We don't want to repeat an endless cycle from mindlessness to mindfulness without ever experiencing a mindset upgrade.

To have an impact, we can't stop at mindfulness. We can't just separate ourselves from our circumstances. We have to engage with the circumstances we face and engage without insecurity. Leaders who lead for impact don't just distance themselves from the thoughts, emotions, and feelings they experience. They distance themselves *so* they can clearly assess what is troubling them, evaluate their motives, and determine the right action.

Remember the story about me almost texting my daughter after she asked me not to use her room without permission? At that moment, I became mindful that I was about to fire a text at her out of insecurity. The mindset upgrade happened when I became aware that she has a space, cares for it, and is learning to be independent. Mindfulness interrupted the insecurity. A mindset upgrade helped me determine the next right action to take.

These small moments of mindfulness transforming into a mindset upgrade have changed my life. I become mindful I'm washing the dishes for validation. A mindset upgrade occurs when I serve without being noticed. I become mindful that I want the board to think I'm awesome. A mindset upgrade occurs when I know where I'm leading us next. I become mindful that I want you to believe this is the best leadership book you've ever read. A mindset upgrade occurs as I write to impact you, not for my validation. Living from a mindset upgrade doesn't mean I act out of perfectly pure motives 100% of the time. It means that at any given moment, I act at least 51% or greater with a motivation to serve others more than myself.

Leaders who lead for impact use mindfulness to assess the motives behind their actions and weigh their values. They use mindfulness to transform their insecurities into a mindset upgrade that inspires the right action with the right motive, changing lives and changing the world.

CHAPTER 7

EMPATHY IS FOR THE PSYCHOTIC

The second way modern leadership development distorts the SightShift Impact Formula™ is by emphasizing empathy as a job well done for leaders. It's not wrong. It's just incomplete.

Empathy is important. As leaders, we want to be in tune with our feelings and the feelings of others. If we're entirely divorced from emotions, we'll miss the purpose and joy behind our actions. We'll become emotionally dead and erode from within. We also don't want to be dominated by our emotions so much that they cloud our judgment. We want to act with wisdom. We want to be aware of and learn from our emotions. But empathy alone isn't enough to make us leaders of impact.

Empathy alone is for the psychotic religious leaders, politicians, and people at work who know how to fake emotion to manipulate you for their purpose. They express empathy as an action to absolve themselves of your suffering. When empathy is the finish line of our actions, our actions become about us and our validation. If we only empathize with the people we care about most when they are suffering, then we are indifferent to the real impact of leadership.

To lead for impact, you can't just *feel* the pain of others. You have to take action to end their suffering. You have to bring solutions to problems. If your house burns down in a fire, the neighbor looking out her window feeling bad for you has sympathy but doesn't help solve the problem. The co-worker telling you a story about how it happened to them has empathy for your struggle but doesn't help solve the problem. The neighbor next door, who lets you sleep in their guest room until you can get things back in order, has a solution to the problem. This person has mercy.

Sympathy is feeling bad *for* someone. Empathy is feeling bad *with* someone. Mercy is taking action to end their suffering.

The modern definition of mercy emphasizes withholding punishment, but the word's true origin focuses on ending suffering. True mercy occurs when someone with the power and resources to make you whole again does something to end your suffering.

For example, consider the manager who overcommits herself until she reaches the edge of burnout. Mercy isn't when her boss lowers the standards and absolves her of her responsibility. Mercy is when her boss takes something off her plate to relieve the short-term suffering and then helps her develop the skills to prioritize her work for the future.

Or consider the doctor who has been sober for a decade but then becomes so overwhelmed by the appointments on his schedule that he gives in to a bottle of vodka. Mercy isn't when the hospital administration looks the other way and doesn't punish him for his declining performance. Mercy is when the hospital administration flies him to a rehab center and covers his appointments while he gets the help he needs.

Empathy doesn't change lives. Taking action to end someone's suffering does. That doesn't mean empathy has no value. In many contexts, empathy is enough. The real value of empathy comes when we use it as a clue to where we can apply mercy. The things that provoke our empathetic emotions provide direction for where we can take action. To be a leader of impact, we don't stop at the emotional feeling; we carry that through to action.

One construction company we worked with had a client who invested in a development project. The client had a location downtown in the path of protests that were occurring through the city. The construction company was afraid rioters would destroy property and possibly ruin livelihoods with their damage. They felt bad for their client. But they didn't stop at empathy. They took action. They used their own resources to board up the windows and protect the client's investment. They exhibited what it means to lead for impact.

You can have sympathy for a lot of people. You can have empathy for some. But you can have mercy for only a few. The world has an overwhelming number of problems to solve, and technology has allowed us to connect to more suffering than ever before. It's more than any individual can solve. We can't end all the world's suffering and shouldn't try. And not everyone wants us to end their suffering. (This is especially true in personal and romantic relationships.) But we can assess where we are right now, notice where we feel empathy, consider what we value and the impact we seek to make, and find a way to end suffering. This mindset has been the driving force behind many of the most impactful businesses we've worked with. A leader felt the suffering of others and took action to end it.

You might think your work is too insignificant to be considered a mercy-based mission or that you aren't ending anyone's suffering. Maybe you're not ending suffering because you're trying to solve *too many* problems. Your lack of focus and commitment is your way of leading for validation. Maybe you're hesitant to put yourself out there or can't muster the courage necessary to have a life-changing impact on someone's life. It's also possible that's just the voice of your insecurity.

You don't need to be in a high-ranking position or a large company to fulfill a mission that changes people's lives. You just need to understand how true transformation works. It doesn't happen at the macro level from the top down. It happens from the ground up through small micro-communities. It happens within your team and through the team you lead.

Likely, the most common form of suffering the people on your team face is the insecurity they feel in their relationships at work and home. They're suffering from a lack of meaning and purpose. They're suffering from the doubts they have about who they are. You can help end their suffering through the environment you create. You can help them find meaning and purpose in what they do. You can help them face their doubts and raise their level of excellence. Doing so will require an environment not built on psychological safety alone. It will require an environment that uses psychological safety to raise the standards and help them grow.

CHAPTER 8

WE'RE STUCK IN PUBERTY

The third way modern leadership development distorts the SightShift Impact Formula™ is by making psychological safety the driving motive of healthy environments.

So many environments fail to impact because leaders focus more on avoiding discomfort than on pursuing growth and excellence. We lower performance standards, absolve people of responsibility, and protect them from the consequences of their actions so they don't have to face their doubts or feel threatened by their insecurity. As a result, we create environments where everyone lives and leads for their comfort and validation rather than for growth and impact.

You can see this at work in the factions that are emerging within organizations. Workplaces today have become dominated by hyper-specialized committees, each focused on a different point of victimization and demanding to be heard and consented to. The energy required to appease each group becomes draining to the overall mission. The real danger comes with the coddling that keeps each special-interest group looking out for their particular interests. They become validation committees, not impact committees.

Don't get me wrong. There are real problems in society, and people are experiencing real pain. I'm not dismissing or discounting this. But how we address these issues isn't helping us grow and advance. It's like we've created an environment that has normalized capable adults sitting in high chairs banging on their trays to be fed, taken care of, cleaned up after, and given whatever they want. It's keeping us stuck in a victimized mindset. What is emerging is not just a workplace issue. It's a societal issue that we can trace back over 100 years ago to the introduction of adolescence.

Adolescence, as we've created it, is a multi-year period beginning with puberty, during which a person is supposed to "find themselves." It's a concept unique to the human species. It doesn't exist anywhere else in nature. When Momma Bird pushes Baby Bird out of the nest, Baby Bird doesn't have a multi-year period to discover who it is and find meaning. It's fly or die.

I'm not saying humans need to be as barbaric as animals, and I'm not saying puberty isn't a real thing. I'm the father of three daughters. I've experienced first-hand the extremes of this transition. So much changes in our brains chemically as the intensity of hormones escalates. It's a real struggle, and we momentarily lose our minds. But we've bastardized this stage of the development process and, in a sense, kept us all stuck in puberty.

For centuries, societies used rituals at the onset of puberty to guide young people through their transition to adulthood, as discussed in Chapter 4. These rituals anchored what was changing in them and gave them an identity, meaning, and purpose. But early in the 20th century, people turned adolescence into a multi-year, open-ended experience of self-discovery. Rather than a two or three-day ritual that gives us an identity shift, we set aside a two or three-year period for young people to wallow in their insecurity as they experience these drastic changes. And it's only getting worse.

We extended this two-to-three-year period through high school and our teenage years. Then, we extended it again through college. Recently, the American Psychology Association lengthened adolescence to 25 years old. They did this in response to modern science, which discovered that the brain continues to experience significant changes up to 25 years old. That doesn't mean we should reduce pressure until the brain finishes changing.

It doesn't take a brain scientist to see this approach isn't working. If you met an 18-year-old in the 1800s, you likely met a mature, functioning adult. If you meet an 18-year-old today, are you meeting a mature, functioning adult? Probably not. What happens when we start excusing behavior, saying, "What do you expect? They're only 24 years old!" When will it ever end?

Mental health suffering today is off the charts, but it's not because life has become more difficult. Sure, we have different challenges now, and we are exposed to more of the world's stress and pressure than ever before, but extending adolescence hasn't better prepared us to face these challenges and pressures. Instead, it has made us more fragile.

To deal with this fragility, we have prioritized psychological safety as the most crucial part of a healthy culture. Psychological safety is necessary, but we've misapplied it. Instead of taking a leadership approach to our challenges that helps people grow, we've overemphasized a therapeutic approach that disempowers them. While psychology wrestles with how to classify mental health struggles, the therapeutic speak that has crept into organizations has everyone seeking a label for their struggle. We then attach these labels to our identity, trapping us in a victim mindset. We attribute poor results to what we perceive as unchangeable defects and settle for less than we're capable of. Of course, people do experience real struggles with depression, anxiety, and the different ways our brains work. The point isn't to disavow the struggle. The point is to build an environment where we can grow in the struggle. The labels we use can help or hurt depending on what we do with them. We can use them as an excuse to lower standards, or we can use them to explain why and how we will advance differently.

When we are insecure as leaders, we feel a burden to rescue our team from their struggles in the name of psychological safety. We feel pressure to shield them from the results so the hard truth of reality doesn't shake them. We cover up their mistakes so they aren't humiliated. We withhold honest feedback so they aren't offended. We lower the demands so we don't demean them. Our intentions are good, but it's stunting their growth.

Coddling produces an ineptness that doesn't prepare us to survive, much less thrive. If Momma Bird over-cares for her young, then nature will destroy them. The bird that can't fly or hunt doesn't eat. The bird that doesn't eat doesn't survive. Bye-bye, Baby Bird. It is Momma Bird's responsibility to prepare her young to survive, and it is our responsibility as leaders and parents to prepare our young to thrive. We don't do that by coddling them.

When we lead for impact, we don't use psychological safety to overprotect our team. We use it as a vehicle for growth. We encourage mistakes and allow people to feel the results without drowning in the consequences. We protect them from car wrecks while letting them feel the sting of bike wrecks until they are ready to drive the car themselves. We acknowledge their insecurity while raising the standards. We affirm personhood while correcting performance.

Demanding more from the people we lead is not demeaning. It's empowering. Confronting them with the reality of their results isn't offensive. It fosters long-term growth. Making mistakes isn't humiliating. It's how we develop humility. This is the pathway to growth.

Real growth happens when we take risks, make mistakes, and feel the feedback of tangible results. It happens when we face challenges that stir up our doubts and when we face those doubts head-on. Feeling doubt is not a mental health crisis. It's a clue to where we feel insecure. When we discover that who we are is not defined by the results of our performance, we experience an identity shift. We shed victim labels and grow into our full potential. We become leaders who lead for impact, not validation.

To be clear, there are scenarios when therapy is an effective approach and times when it is the best solution. Therapy has transformed people I know and helped me. However, for many people, therapy has become a destination rather than a stepping stone to a thriving life. Rather than using it as a tool to build skills, it becomes a mindset they never graduate from. When we take a leadership approach to our challenges, we root out the rot in our mindset and continue growing.

As we grow and advance, we experience new doubts. These doubts reveal deeper insecurities, which reveal where we need an identity shift. It's a process to stay hungry for and one that's never finished. When we stop feeling doubts, we become complacent, lose our curiosity, and stop growing. Unfortunately, this has become the reality for so many people.

Society has conditioned young people to put off adulthood as long as possible in favor of the risk-free, fantastical adventure of discovering oneself. Then, they are encouraged to settle into a salaried career, shielded from the invaluable lessons that come from risk and reward. This path disconnects them from consequential feedback that incites growth, and they wander in the wilderness, trying to find themselves.

We don't need a multi-year period where we are protected from all risks and absolved of all responsibility while "finding ourselves." We need purpose, direction, and an environment that pushes us to grow. We don't need a month-long backpacking trip through Europe to discover who we are. We need to share in the wins and losses of a collective pursuit and own the responsibility for our contributions. We don't need psychological safety to coddle us into a victim mindset. We need psychological safety to allow us to wrestle with our doubts while we pursue greatness.

The world doesn't need more mindless doers who are safe and protected. The world needs more secure leaders who are hungry for growth; leaders who launch from the nest and learn to fly, hunt, and thrive; leaders who lead with courage and kindness; leaders who know how to affirm the person and raise the standard; leaders who know how to take the right action with the right motive to make a lasting impact; and leaders who can help others do the same.

To become that kind of leader, we must learn a process that guides us to lead for impact over and over again, in every moment, big and small. A process that helps us become a world-class leader of impact.

PART 3

BECOMING A WORLD-CLASS LEADER

CHAPTER 9
THE DEFINITION OF WORLD-CLASS LEADERSHIP

Whether leading a family or leading a team at work, the leadership journey constantly shapes us. It has the potential to stimulate deep self-understanding and self-mastery. It can be a transformative process and a catalyst for mastering skills, discovering purpose, and truly growing and developing.

Unfortunately, most work environments have devolved into corporate drudgery focused on reading every email and accepting every meeting invite to distract us from dealing with real issues. Most family environments have become micromanaged daycares, content to keep everyone busy, entertained, and out of trouble. Most leadership development has become surface-level spectacles that don't transform who we are. We've sterilized fertile developmental ground and lost sight of what matters most: developing leaders. As a result, we're creating serviceable managers but lousy leaders, and frankly, managing people is exhausting.

It's exhausting to nag your team or kids to get them to follow through on their commitments, pressure them to meet expectations, manipulate them to keep them engaged, and try to avoid confrontation, hoping it will all work itself out. No one enjoys managing people, but that's what we have been trained to do. It's time to change that.

It's time for us to stop managing and start leading, to stop nagging and start developing. It's time for us to help people become the leaders they were meant to be: leaders who lead for impact, not validation.

Tools and technology will continue to advance to the point that software and AI will fulfill our management needs, but technology can't replace the power of leading people. Developing leaders who can develop other leaders is a different end goal than most people even consider.

When you look back 20 years from now, your satisfaction won't come from answering all your emails, accepting every meeting invite, or from how many extracurricular activities your kids participate in. Your satisfaction will come from who you became on the leadership journey and who you helped others become. How you respond in the moments you feel insecure will determine who you become.

When you face moments of doubt, will you take action to serve your needs and comfort your insecurity, or will you take action from a secure identity that ends the suffering of others? Will you express your values in their extremes or balance the values of the whole team?

The next time a team member misses a critical benchmark, forget the gravity of their failure for a moment. Instead, pay attention to what is happening in you. Peel back the anger, irritation, or frustration you feel, regardless of its validity. Go deeper. What does their failure make you feel about who you are as a leader? Without awareness, you will likely respond in a way that takes control of the situation and manipulates it for your benefit. It will make you feel better but make them feel worse. You will lead for validation.

Instead, be mindful of the insecurity surfacing inside you and transform it with a mindset upgrade. Consider your motive and connect it to your doubt. Perhaps this team member has taken advantage of your graciousness in the past, or you feel like they're holding you back, so your first reaction is to protect yourself. But if your motive is about you, it will deform you. You aren't developing yourself or them.

Next, be empathetic toward the circumstances that led to their mistake. Ask them to explain why they missed the deadline. Put yourself in their shoes. Seek to understand before being understood. But don't stop there. With mercy, take action to end their suffering.

Finally, use psychological safety to help them own their mistake and grow from it. Affirm personhood before correcting their performance so they don't power up back at you or withdraw and hide, never solving the real problem.

Awareness of when you feel insecure will start you on the path of impact.

If we don't learn how to properly order the internal pressure and doubts we feel from pursuing our ambition, we will turn toward leading for validation. We will take the wrong action with the wrong motive. Over time, our actions will create a culture of an entire company, team, or family pursuing validation.

Culture is not the words we say or the values we post on the website. It's not built through trust falls, gimmicky seminars, or trendy office setups. It's not established through ideological conformity. Culture is created by the actions we consistently take, especially in moments of stress, pressure, and transition, when we and the people we lead feel the most insecure. Mastering the SightShift Impact Formula™ will keep us on the path of impact.

When we follow the SightShift Impact Formula™, we take action from a secure identity with the motive to serve others, and we balance the values of the whole team. As a result, we create a culture of leaders who can develop other leaders of impact, which separates world-class leaders from everyone else.

A great leader is not the one who gets the most done or the one who people like the most. It's not the loudest person in the room or the most disciplined. It's not the one with the best education or pedigree. It's not the one with the largest team, portfolio, or revenue. It's not the youngest. It's not the oldest. It's not the male. It's not the female.

Three simple things define a world-class leader:

1. They are secure in who they are.
2. They are clear in their mission.
3. They build and attract healthy community.

When you have experienced an identity shift and come to know who you are, you can make meaning out of even the worst of circumstances. With a secure identity, it becomes clear what you are to do, and you can determine what direction to go and what action to take, even during times of chaos and confusion. With this clarity in direction, you can build healthy community by continually renewing relationships even when people are frustrating and hard to deal with. Most importantly, world-class leaders who meet this standard can develop other leaders who can do the same.

Becoming a leader of impact is not an overnight transformation. It is a daily commitment and a lifelong pursuit. Your journey down that path will shape who you become and who you help others become. It can make you a better version of who you are or a worse version of who you are. And through your leadership, you can help others become a better or worse version of themselves.

To ensure you become a leader of impact, you need a process that systemizes your leadership development. We've built a system for you that develops leaders who can develop leaders that are secure in who they are, clear in their mission, and build healthy community. It has helped all ranges of companies, from small businesses to mid-market growth companies to Fortune 100 companies, accomplish the most ambitious growth goals by developing world-class leaders who develop other leaders. And it does it in four hours per month or less. It's called the SightShift Leadership Operating System™.

CHAPTER 10

A LEADERSHIP OPERATING SYSTEM

No one becomes a world-class leader just because they want to. In most cases, people don't rise to the level of their hopes; they sink to the level of their training. Greatness, wherever it's found, whether in sports, in art, or in leadership, isn't the result of fluke happenstance. It is conditioned through systems.

Athletes use systems to stay disciplined in training regimens to prepare for the biggest moments. Musicians use systems to learn and master chords to improvise beautiful melodies. Writers use systems to generate and synthesize new ideas. Unfortunately, most leadership development doesn't use the same approach.

Most people and companies piecemeal their leadership development haphazardly. They approach it like a hot air balloon, filled with inspiration and hype but unable to withstand the swirling winds. As things change or adversity hits, the plans come crashing down. Or they approach it like a circus. They go through the motions and keep the show going but don't change lives. Or they approach it like a leaky ship, full steam ahead, but unaware of the cracks beneath the surface dragging it down.

To become a world-class leader, you need a system that anchors your transformation through an identity shift. To develop a team of leaders, you need a system that makes leadership development a repeatable, sustainable process. To create a culture of leadership development in your organization, you need a system that can fix any leadership issues before those issues sink your ship.

If you want to develop leaders who develop other leaders, you need the SightShift Leadership Operating System™.

The SightShift Leadership Operating System™

Becoming world-class in anything is less about the quantity of time spent and more about the quality of time spent. It's the combination of giving your full attention and effort to the highest leveraged practices. The busiest, most ambitious leaders don't have time to sacrifice multiple hours a week on development seminars, and the SightShift LOS™ has proven that's unnecessary.

The SightShift LOS™ encapsulates everything necessary to develop leaders of impact and makes their development predictable, repeatable, and scalable. It's designed to keep your curiosity and imagination engaged on the path to becoming a leader of impact. And it's formatted to develop leaders in four hours a month or less.

It doesn't approach leadership development like a hot air balloon, a circus, or a leaky ship. It's not built on hype that crumbles in the face of adversity, it doesn't include surface-level entertainment that doesn't last, and it doesn't cover up cracks in the foundation but exposes them. The SightShift LOS™ follows the model of "Be The Tree."

The fruit of the tree represents the culture. Like fruit doesn't attach itself to a tree, you can't force culture onto an organization. Instead, an organization produces culture out of the overflow of a healthy leadership environment. The SightShift LOS™ doesn't force a cultural framework onto your organization. It provides a process to help you build a customized cultural playbook unique to your industry and goals. This playbook becomes the map that makes your culture sustainable and scalable as you grow.

The trunk of the tree represents the skills that turn managers into leaders. Culture isn't transformed from the top down. It is transformed through micro-apprenticeships. In this phase of the SightShift LOS™, leaders are trained in a coaching process that guides people through an identity shift, introduces the tools, frameworks, and processes that become the common language and daily practices of the organization, and helps every individual in the organization actively build the culture they want to be a part of.

The root of the tree represents the part of the SightShift LOS™ that seeds the transformation. It's the part that strengthens the trunk and nourishes the fruit. Most leadership development skips over this unseen part of how people grow and develop. Most leadership development sells the fruit because that's what everyone can see, but it doesn't last. When they promise to fix the fruit but don't transform the roots, the culture won't sustain the changes through the usual drift and distraction every organization and leader experiences.

Installing a leadership operating system that transforms your culture requires more than just introducing new tools, teaching skills, or adopting the latest leadership principles. It requires more than a communication framework or a meeting structure. Giving a tool to an insecure leader doesn't mean they have the skills to execute it well. Teaching a skill to an insecure leader doesn't mean they have the mindset to apply the skill effectively. A leadership operating system that genuinely transforms the culture transforms the people. To transform the people it has to transform the root of who they are. If your personal or team growth plan doesn't include an identity shift, it won't get you where you want to be. That's why, for the first time in the history of leadership development, we created a tool that makes it possible to measure what is happening at the root of your leaders and organization. It's called the Identity Fear Quotient™.

The Identity Fear Quotient™

The Identity Fear Quotient™ is a proprietary measurement tool created by SightShift™ that produces a datatized view of what is happening at the core of who you are and your organization. It peeks beneath the surface to reveal the truth about your insecurities and how they impact your leadership.

All effective transformation begins with an honest look in the mirror, but it's hard to get honest feedback. Most people are so consumed with their insecurities that they can't see you for who you are or your full potential. Their own proving and hiding cloud their measurement. 360-degree reviews have not and will not transform leaders because everyone evaluates others through their insecurities. And most of the assessment tools we use to gain a better understanding of people are incomplete. They tell you *what* you do but don't tell you *why* you do it. They may tell your co-workers how to communicate with you, but they don't help you understand why you receive feedback the way you do. They may tell you where you derive energy from but don't reveal where or how you seek validation and sabotage your leadership. They may identify your strengths but don't tell you how you overvalue them and create an unbalanced culture.

Assessments that constrain us in a box, reduce us to a label, or tell us what we already know about ourselves don't help us grow. The most valuable measurement tools uncover the defense mechanisms we use to mask our insecurities and expand us into new consciousness. That is the power of the IFQ™.

The IFQ™ doesn't just assess personality and assign labels. It explores the depths of who you are. It reveals where you are most insecure and how your insecurities shape your culture. It forecasts where your biggest struggles will come from and how you unknowingly sabotage your leadership impact. It raises the awareness of every leader in the organization, beginning with the leadership team, because if they don't experience this transformation, the rest of the organization won't either. They can't give what they don't have.

After sitting with so many teams and reviewing the results of their IFQ™, a funny pattern has emerged. As we review the profiles of each team member, the leader will nod in agreement like we are giving words to what they have known intuitively all along. Then, we get to the leader's profile. As we interpret the results, their eyes will squint, their lips will purse, and their head will shake ever so slightly. "Wow. I was impressed. You nailed everyone else, but this doesn't describe me." As they say this, I notice other team members rolling their eyes at the lack of awareness. Some of them even chuckle. It's hard to see clearly without a mirror. It's like being at dinner and seeing the poppy seed stuck between someone else's teeth but not noticing the giant spinach dangling from your own. You need a mirror to clearly see what is happening in your own root system before you can truly impact someone else. The IFQ™ is that mirror and is the first step in becoming a leader of impact.

* * *

At this point, I would typically close with a story that leaves you breathless and teary-eyed, inspired to take the next step, but frankly, the world is tired, and people are exhausted. I believe that we would all just like to exist in an environment that is more insulated from all the insanity of politics, generational differences, invasive technology,and overwhelming suffering of the world. We don't need more hype or persuasion. We need a better way.

We need more healthy leaders who are secure in who they are. We need more leaders who don't coddle a victim mindset. We need more leaders who know their identity is more than any single marker. We need more leaders who have experienced an identity shift, can show up with clarity in their mission, and can build healthy community.

How the world approaches leadership right now isn't working. Modern leadership development isn't serving us well. It's not building world-class leaders. Too many leaders lead for validation, not impact, and insecure leaders ruin the world.

We need a better way to leverage the moments we have to become the leaders we are meant to become.

We need to choose a different path.

A more complete path.

A path of impact.

IMPACT = RIGHT ACTION + RIGHT MOTIVE

Do you know what's keeping you from becoming a great leader?

Do you have a roadmap to get there?

Too many leaders lead for validation, not impact.
(And most don't even realize they're doing it!)

As a result, it sabotages their effectiveness, strains their relationships, and they fall short of their potential.

We don't want to see that happen to you!

Whether you lead a team or a family, we've helped hundreds of leaders like you become leaders of impact using the **Identity Fear Quotient™**.

The IFQ™ is a 6-question measurement tool that reveals how and why you lead for validation under stress and provides a customized roadmap to help you finally become the leader you were meant to be.

It's not too late to become a leader of impact.

Begin your transformational leadership journey today.

TAKE THE IFQ™ AT WWW.SIGHTSHIFT.COM/IFQ

About the Authors

Dr. Chris McAlister

Dr. Chris McAlister is an author, speaker, and leadership coach based in Columbus, Ohio. He is the founder of SightShift, a leadership development company that helps company owners achieve their 3-5 year goals by developing leaders at scale. He's authored eight books on leadership development and loves helping ambitious, values based people become the leaders they were meant to be. Chris has delivered his transformational process globally to leaders of various industries, including small and mid-market company founders, physicians, Fortune 100 executives, venture fund managers, serial entrepreneurs, professional athletes, and nonprofit directors. He also trains others to coach through this process as well. You can become the leader you were meant to be at SightShift.com.

Bret Burchard

Coach Bret is a professional author, speaker, and coach. He is the co-founder of ChampionShift, a mindset training company that helps athletes and coaches compete and lead with confidence, resilience, and humility. He has co-authored seven books on mindset and leadership development, including *Catching Confetti: Developing the Mindset of a Champion* and *Figure That Shift Out: An Invitation to Relax Into Your Brilliance.* You can learn to develop the mind of a champion at ChampionShift.com.

Made in the USA
Columbia, SC
27 November 2024

47248365R00043